MW01153154

This Book Belongs To:

Mario Brewer

The Story of
ALONZO HERNDON
Who Says a Slave Can't be a Millionaire?

By
Adam Herndon

Illustrated by
Jamie Rachal

ISBN: 0615753027
ISBN 13: 9780615753027

*Dedicated to the beautiful women in my life who have inspired me
to believe in myself and always strive for greatness.
Thank you mom, grandma, Aunt Brenda,
Cousin Cathy and my lovely wife Chandra.*

The Story of
ALONZO HERNDON
Who Says a Slave Can't be a Millionaire?

"Cock-a-doodle-doo, cock-a-doodle-doo". Alonzo knew that sound very well. It meant that he had to end his pleasant dream, open his eyes and wake up and start a new day. The calling of the roosters every morning signaled that it was time to begin his daily chores.

1

Feed the chickens, milk the cows.
Don't forget the field to plow.
All of that lay ahead of him and the sun hadn't even risen yet.
This is not the life for a kid, Alonzo used to think to himself as he'd wipe the sleep from his eyes.

Alonzo Herndon was born on a farm in Georgia during a time when people were judged by their skin color and not by the type of person they were on the inside. He and his family were slaves and were owned by the owners of the farm where they lived. They were forced to work long, hard days out in the fields under the blazing sun and were never given any money for all of their exhausting labor.

When Alonzo turned six, he was told that he was now old enough to go out into the fields and work alongside his family. This was very confusing to Alonzo because it was the last thing in the world that he wanted to do. It was no fun at all! He didn't

3

understand why he couldn't go to school like other kids his age and why he and his family were treated so mean. His confusion made him very sad. Sometimes he'd cry himself to sleep at night. Eventually, his tears turned into anger. "This isn't fair!" he used to vent to his mother. He told his mom everything, letting her know that it made no sense to him that other people got to enjoy themselves but all it seemed that he and his family ever had to do was work, work and more work.

But it never did any good or changed their situation. His mom tried to explain to him that some things about life just don't seem to make sense sometimes and that there was nothing that they could do to change their circumstances.

Alonzo told his mother that he dreamed of running away. But she warned him that they might be hurt if they tried to run away. So they stayed. Their difficult life — making someone else rich while they did all the work — continued the same as always.

With no other hope in sight, Alonzo looked up to the stars every night and prayed that one day life would be different and everyone would be treated fairly. "God," the little boy would say, "I know You can do it." And he had faith that He would.

When Alonzo was seven his prayers were answered. He would never forget that magical morning when he woke up and his mom told him the most amazing, awesome news ever: the President of the United States passed a law stating that slavery was wrong and was no longer allowed. Alonzo and his family – along with all of the other slaves throughout the land – rejoiced and celebrated their freedom! "Hip-hip hooray!" Alonzo shouted as he danced in circles. He was so happy that he didn't have to work on the farm anymore and was free to play and have fun. He had to pinch himself to make sure he wasn't dreaming.

7

Unfortunately, Alonzo found out that even though he and his family were free, life wasn't going to be as fun as he thought. After leaving the farm where they had toiled for all those years, they did not have any money nor did they have a place to stay. Sadly, there was no time for fun and games for Alonzo because he would have to work to help out his family.

Still, Alonzo was glad that he didn't have to work on that farm anymore and now he had a chance to find out exactly what he could do with his life now that he and his family were free.

As he grew up, while other kids went to school, Alonzo had to work doing odd jobs like selling peanuts and molasses to earn money. He was always careful to save a small amount of his money, setting it aside in a secret place so that someday in the future he could use it to do something to make his life better. It seemed like a small amount at first but Alonzo remembered a wise old saying he had had once heard somewhere: "A penny saved is a penny earned."

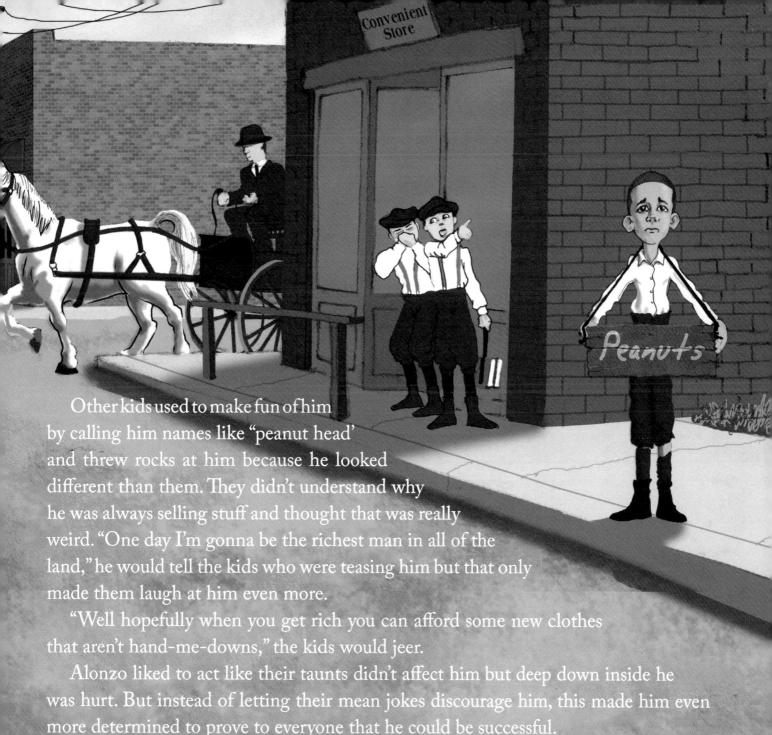

Other kids used to make fun of him
by calling him names like "peanut head"
and threw rocks at him because he looked
different than them. They didn't understand why
he was always selling stuff and thought that was really
weird. "One day I'm gonna be the richest man in all of the
land," he would tell the kids who were teasing him but that only
made them laugh at him even more.

"Well hopefully when you get rich you can afford some new clothes
that aren't hand-me-downs," the kids would jeer.

Alonzo liked to act like their taunts didn't affect him but deep down inside he
was hurt. But instead of letting their mean jokes discourage him, this made him even
more determined to prove to everyone that he could be successful.

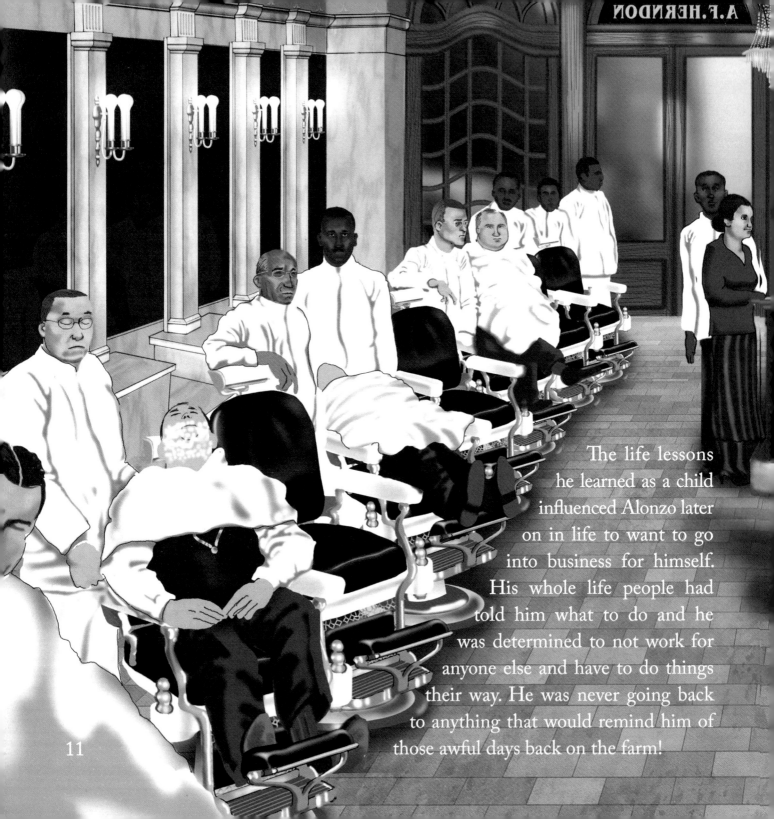

The life lessons he learned as a child influenced Alonzo later on in life to want to go into business for himself. His whole life people had told him what to do and he was determined to not work for anyone else and have to do things their way. He was never going back to anything that would remind him of those awful days back on the farm!

11

With the money that he saved, he bought a pair of hair clippers and learned how to cut hair. Through hard work he was able to achieve his dream of owning his own business by opening his own barbershop. He named it the Crystal Palace and it became the world's biggest and best barbershop. Finally, his hard work was paying off for him!

12

Even though Alonzo no longer struggled, he never forgot about the hard life he had growing up poor. He knew that he now had an opportunity to make a real difference in the world and he wanted to help people whose lives were not as fortunate as his. Using the money he earned from his barbershop, Alonzo bought old houses, fixed them up and rented them out for affordable prices to people who did not have a lot of money.

These folks were so grateful that a man with a big heart actually cared enough to want to help them. And Alonzo was grateful for the chance to be able to do it because it made him feel good inside to see how happy they were.

Alonzo Herndon went on to do even more good deeds. He later founded Atlanta Life Insurance to help less fortunate families during times when they were sick or in the hospital.

Daily World

15

Because of his good work towards others, people trusted in him. Like a boomerang, all of the good things that Alonzo had done for people came back to him in an even bigger way. He was able to turn his small local company into one of the biggest companies in America.

His dream had come true! The boy who started off his life as a slave working the fields was now a wealthy business owner – and for the rest of his life he did whatever he could to try to help other people achieve their dreams too.

ABOUT THE AUTHOR

Adam Herndon spent his childhood in Oakland, CA and currently is an insurance agent and business owner in Laurel, MD. He is the great, great nephew of Alonzo Herndon and current Board of Trustee Member of The Alonzo F. Herndon Foundation. He has served as Chairman of the Board at University Community Academy, featured on Fox 5 'Good Day Atlanta', WSB-TV's 'Georgia's Hidden Treasures' and highlighted in Atlanta Tribune, The Magazine for contributions to the community. Adam is a proud graduate of The Ohio State University. He is married to Chandra and has two children, Chase and Jalen.

For more information about the author including book signings and speaking engagements, please visit www.adameherndon.com.

ABOUT THE ILLUSTRATOR

Jamie Rachal grew up in Oakland, California where he was inspired and surrounded by fine art as a child. He holds a bachelor's degree in Art and currently works as a graphic designer. In his spare time, Jamie loves playing sports, drawing and painting portraits for professional athletes. He lives in Atlanta, Georgia with his wife and 2 sons, Jason and Cayden.